The Love of My Life Swept Me Off My Feet THE GREAT I AM

(Passing on Inspirations)
By

Gloria Waters

ISBN: 1-4107-2456-5 (e-book)
ISBN: 1-4107-2457-3 (Paperback)

This book is printed on acid free paper.

1st Books - rev. 08/04/03

DEDICATION

I give Honor and Praise to my Lord Jesus Christ who has always, is always, and will always be the Light that Shines Brightly in my Life.

This book is dedicated to a very special person in my life. As a member of Grove Baptist Church, under the leadership of Dr. Melvin O. Marriner my relationship with God the Father, the Son, and the Holy Spirit came alive. Through Dr. Marriner's teachings I learned how to acquire an intimate relationship with God. So on this day of publication I would like to thank Dr. Melvin O. Marriner for all that he has done.

Pastor Marriner, Thank you and from your own words: We are... walking, talking, breathing, living, MIRACLES.

"I Love You to Life."

iv

PREVIEW

This book has three chapters <u>STOP</u>, <u>THINK</u>, and <u>STAND</u>. You see that's all that God wants from us. He wants us to first STOP.

<u>Stop</u> moving all around because you can't fully comprehend that God is trying to tell you something when you're walking, talking, laughing, playing, etc. We need to cease all movement. WE NEED TO HEAR THE VOICE OF GOD!!

<u>Think</u>, this word also means to mediate. Mediate on what God is saying to us, so that we will understand and comprehend his words with clarity. WE NEED TO HEAR THE VOICE OF GOD!!

<u>Stand</u>, the Master said it best "be still." Stop trying to do it, fix it, and work it out. Be lead by the spirit "The Master." He is the movement... "<u>The Holy Ghost Movement</u>." WE NEED TO HEARD THE VOICE OF GOD!!

I heard the voice of God, this is how He... Swept Me Off My Feet. You see, once I stopped to hear God's voice, He gave me clarity in my thought process and then I understood that I needed to stand so He could show me the way.

My bothers and sisters again I say we were created for one purpose… "To Obey God" (love him, worship him, and praise him). Now, how do we do that you say? WE <u>STOP</u> AN TAKE THE TIME TO <u>THINK</u>, THEN JUST <u>STAND</u> AND LET THE MASTER ORDER OUR STEPS.

We all know from one extreme to the other there is…Bad & Good, Dark & Light, and Hell & Heaven (or do we). The latter of these is why this book has been created. To help us maybe understand (in everyday language), how to get from point A to point B. The why, where, when, what, and how God is EVERYTHING to us even when we don't recognize it.

*God is… **Almighty/Everywhere** – Omnipresent*
*God is… **All Powerful/In Control** – Omnipotent*
*God is… - **The Creator of all** – Omniscience*

TABLE OF CONTENTS

ABOUT THE AUTHOR

LIFE- LESSON JOURNAL

PART ONE

Gloria Waters

CHAPTER ONE

What can we really say about STOP, how do we define STOP, why do we need to explain STOP? We need to discuss STOP because it's an essential word in Gods plan. Granted, everyone knows what stop means in the normal sense...(no movement, still, etc.) but in the spiritual sense, there's plenty to say about STOP.

Now, before we begin to focus on this chapters topic, I'd like to take just a few moments to share the reality of why this book was created. Remember John 1:1 ***"In the beginning was the word and the word was with God and the word was God."*** Let us pray...Thank you right now for your grace and your mercy Holy Father. Let us hear now oh God with understanding and wisdom from you. Open our minds so that each of us many comprehend your will for us through this message. Amen.

What is the Word you say, the word is G O D (God), the Master over the entire universe. We also call the bible "Our Word" our set of instructions on how to, where to, who to, when to, and just because… from God. This is the way we get to know God, how we learn to have a relationship with God, become apart of God. Now notice earlier, I never said why instead I said… just because. See "why" is an irrelevant word in reference to God (having no effect whatsoever on the circumstances or situation). Now let's be real for just a moment, project this image in your mind… a human being asking the Supreme being "why." (*See Figure 1-1*)

Figure 1-1

(Human being)

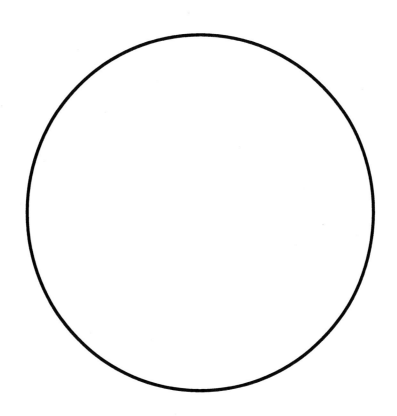

(Supreme being)

Thank you Holy Spirit. This brings to mind a billboard I've seen that states: What Part Of Thou Shall Not Don't You Understand. See if God said it, we're to just do it (I didn't say we'd always like the direction in which the Lord leads us) but if God the Father, the Master of the Universe, the Supreme Being, the one who Created all, is All, and shall Always be... says to do something and we refuse, that is totally detrimental to our entire being. See, we don't truly realize the consequences of being disobedient to God because we don't take the time to STOP and think (which has been man's downfall from the very beginning...act now, think later). It really don't matter how we try to sugar coat it ("oh ah, girl I was so tried" or what about, "see what happen was" or maybe "see for real for real dough"), it still comes out the same (an excuse) for being disobedient to the one who gives us life. Now... I think we all sort of understand why these simple but important words need it be discussed. So, lets now dive right in to STOP!

STOP (cease all movement)

We're all out here singing, "God will fight your battle, God will fight your battle if you just be still" but the truth of the matter is… many of us don't really understand what nor how to *stop* or be still.

You see, from birth until the time we come to know Christ, the world we live in dictates our every move. The word states that we were born into a sinful world, and who is the champion of sin "satan". Now, I've heard some folks say, "don't talk about satan, don't even give him the time of day. Well my brothers and sisters, I'm a firm believer that in order to defeat your opponent you most know something about your opponent. Now if you don't know something about satan's tactic, how he operates, you're already defeated. See, some things you don't know… can hurt you. What makes you think for one moment that satan is going to sit back, quietly and let you come into his territory and understand (with clarity) what's really going on up in here, (Revelation 12:12 states, ***…Woe to the inhabiters of earth and the sea! For the devil is come down unto you, having great wrath because he knoweth that he hath but a short time.***") *KJV*

See his only objective is to still, kill, and destroy you (quickly) so that he will not burn in eternity alone. Don't think that old cliché is just a old wise tale "misery loves company."

You see, we need to wake up and open our eyes so that we can see what God is trying to tell us and until we began to acquire a real relationship with the Master, we will stay clueless to what is really real. Ah! give us clarity Holy Spirit. Remember The Battle of Jericho? God fought the battle but the people had to do their part... be present, praising and worshipping God in. Now I know some of you are about to think I've completely lost my mind when I say this but if you would just hold on and stay with me you'll get this.

If the people wasn't at the battle ground doing their part, God would have done nothing. Ah! I know you're ready to start throwing some spit balls at me now but remember James 2:17... ***"In the same way, faith by itself, if not accompanied by action, is dead."*** *(NIV)* So, we the people must do our part to usher God into our mix, into our lives, to handle the business that we cannot, remember Ephesians 6:12 ***"For we wrestle not against flesh and blood (the body) but against principalities, against powers, against the rulers of darkness of***

this world, against spiritual wickedness in high places" (the evil that controls the body). *KJV*

See only the Spirit can battle the spirit (it's a supernatural thing). If you recall, God had satan thrown out of heaven to earth, where he would deceive the whole world (Revelation 12:9 ***"And the great dragon was cast out, that old serpent called the devil and satan, which deceiveth the whole world..."***) *KJV*. Until God returns with judgement of the world and put a stop to satan's mass destruction of the world, we need to realize that satan is real and powerful (even though we allow him entrance and access). See we think ... "I'm going to allow him just this very minute section of my mind, cause I really want to do this or that (just for a second – to see what it feels like, what it looks like, what it sounds like, etc.). That's all satan needs... to gain entrance into the mind and the body will follow. <u>He is the master infectious disease</u> (AIDS).

> **A** – we <u>A</u>llow
> **I** – he <u>I</u>nfects
> **D** – then <u>D</u>estroys
> **S** – leaves <u>S</u>hallow

Now if you're like me (a visual person), sometimes I need to see what is being said in order to fully grasp the depth of the statement. Look at the illustration below, it should give you a clearer vision of how and what really happens when we allow satan to control us: *See Figure 1-2*

Figure 1-2

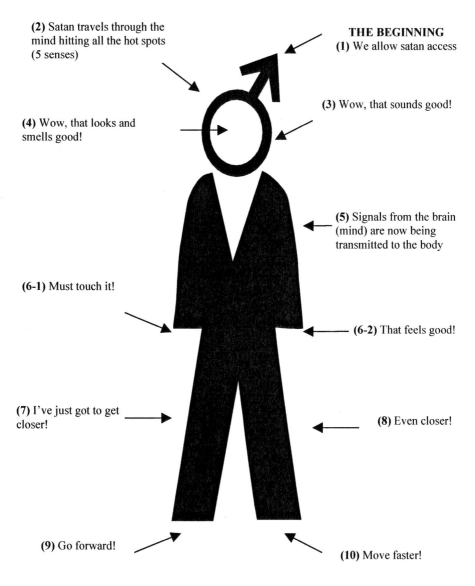

(2) Satan travels through the mind hitting all the hot spots (5 senses)

THE BEGINNING
(1) We allow satan access

(3) Wow, that sounds good!

(4) Wow, that looks and smells good!

(5) Signals from the brain (mind) are now being transmitted to the body

(6-1) Must touch it!

(6-2) That feels good!

(7) I've just got to get closer!

(8) Even closer!

(9) Go forward!

(10) Move faster!

11

See, if you continue to feed the mind with satan's influences eventually the body is left, just a <u>shell</u> of an exterior. My brothers and sisters we need to understand fully why *STOP* is such an importance part of our being. If we don't learn to *stop* (blatantly) allowing satan entrance into our minds we will lose total control of our entire being.

See we need to watch ourselves, take a long look at who and what we really are. If the truth be told… we all need to pray more, study more, trust more and pretend a lot less. See, I know you don't hear me now, cause fantasy is what we want - but reality is what we need. Let's… Get Real!

Psalms 107:2 states, ***"Let the Redeemed of the Lord say so, whom he hath redeemed from the hands of the enemy;" (KJV)*** not the pretender but the redeemed. You see, some of us are still caught up in that old school tradition thing (I can just act like I've been delivered and no one will be the wiser). You know what God says to that… ***STOOOOOP!***

Oh! I'm an Usher but when was the last time we *stopped* to usher God into our lives, to let him use us for his glory without… the church organization being apart of the project. Oh! I'm a Deacon or a

12

Deaconess but when was the last time we *stopped* to assist in helping others without… the church organization being apart of the project. Oh! I'm in this or that ministry but when was the last time we *stopped* to minister to our brothers and sisters on the corner about Jesus without… the church organization being apart of the project. Oh! I'm a Reverend or an Evangelist but when was the last time we *stopped* to direct the young at heart to read the bible without… the church organization being apart of the project. See some of us are still trapped in the church buildings, organizations, and/or traditions. Do you recall **Matthew chapter 23 (The Book)… Then Jesus said to the crowd and his disciples, "The teachers of religious law and the Pharisees are the official interpreters of Scriptures. So practice and obey whatever they say to you,but don't follow their examples. For they don't practice what they teach. They crush you with impossible religious demands and never lift a finger to help ease the burden.**

Everything they do is for show. On their arms they wear extra wide prayer boxes with Scriptures verses inside and they wear extra long tassels on their robes. And how they love to sit at the head table at banquets and in the most prominent seats

in the synagogue! They enjoy the attention they get on the street, and they enjoy being called Rabbi. Don't ever let anyone call you "Rabbi," for you have only one teacher, and all of you are on the same level as brothers and sisters. And don't address anyone here on earth as "Father," for only God in heaven is your spiritual Father. And don't let anyone call you "Master," for there is only one master, the messiah. The greatest among you must be a servant. But those who exalt themselves will be humbled, and those who humble themselves will be exalted.

How terrible it will be for you teachers of religious law and you Pharisees. Hypocrites! For you won't let others enter the kingdom of Heaven, and you won't go in yourselves. Yes, how terrible it will be for you teachers if religious law and you Pharisees. For you cross land and sea to make one convert, and then you turn him into twice the son of hell as you yourselves are.

Blind guides! How terrible it will be for you! For you say that it means nothing to swear by "God's Temple"- you can break that oath. But then you say that it is binding to swear "by the gold in the Temple." Blind fools! Which is greater, the gold, or the Temple that makes the gold sacred? And you say that to take an oath "by the altar" can be broken, but to swear "by the gifts on the altar" is binding! How blind! For which is greater, the gift on the altar, or the altar that makes the gift sacred? When you swear "by the altar," you are swearing by it and by everything on it. And when you swear "by the Temple'" you are swearing by it and God, who lives in it. And when you swear "by heaven," you are swearing by the throne of God and by God, who sits in the throne.

How terrible it will be for you teachers of religious law and you Pharisees. Hypocrites! For you are careful to tithe even the tiniest part of your income, but you ignore the important things of the law-justice, mercy, an faith. You should tithe, yes, but you should not leave undone the more important things. Blind guides! You strain your water so you won't accidentally swallow a gnat; then you swallow a camel!

How terrible it will be for you teachers of religious law and you Pharisees. Hypocrites! You are so careful to clean the outside of the cup and the dish, but inside you are filthy-full of greed and self-indulgence! Blind Pharisees! First wash the inside of the cup, and then the outside will become clean too.

How terrible it will be for you teachers of religious law and Pharisees. Hypocrites! You are like whitewashed tombs-beautiful on the outside but filled on the inside with dead people's bones and all sorts of impurity. You try to look like upright people outwardly, but inside your hearts so filled with hypocrisy and lawlessness.

How terrible it will be for you teachers of religious law and Pharisees. Hypocrites! For you build tombs for the prophets your ancestors killed and decorate the graves of the godly people your ancestors destroyed. Then you sat, "We never would have joined them in killing the prophets."

In saying that, you are accusing yourselves of being the descendants of those who murdered the prophets. Go ahead. Finish what they started. Snakes! Sons of vipers! How will you escape the judgement of hell? I will send you prophets and wise men and teachers of religious law. You will kill some by crucifixion and whip others in your synagogues, chasing them from city to city. As a result, you will become guilty of murdering all the godly people from righteous Abel to Zechariah son of Barachiah, whom you murdered in the Temple between the altar and the sanctuary. I assure you, all the accumulated judgment of the centuries will break upon the head of the very generation.

O Jerusalem, Jerusalem, the city that kills the prophets and stone God's messengers! How often I have wanted to gather your children together as a

hen protects her chicks beneath her wings, but you
wouldn't let me. And now look, your house is left
to you, empty and desolate. For I tell you this, you
will never see me again until you say, "Bless the
one who comes in the name of the Lord!"... this
entire chapters warns us about pretending, listen to
the good that is spoken but do not the evil which is
done. Jesus warns several times in this chapter about
hypocrites, blind guides and blind fools. God is
saying, "Let's just *stop* and get free of <u>all</u> that type
mentality. God is not trapped in a box, a buildings,
an organizations, traditions, etc.), He is with us...
<u>ALWAYS!</u> Now don't misunderstand my brothers
and sisters, yes we have the power of God with us in
a group setting but we also have the
power...**ALONE.** Remember the Word (God), *"I*
can do all things through Christ Jesus who
strengthens me" NIV (Philippians 4:13). Did we get
that? I can...me, myself, singular! See, we don't
always need a group to work for God, we can do
things right by ourselves (as long as we have the
Spirit of God with us) Hallelujah to the Lamb.

God the Father is tried of all this... I'm doing
my own thing because this is what I think God
means—servants, the Master wants some...

follow my commands and do my will—servants. Brothers and sisters, God says it's time to *stop*... playing church. It's time out for doing this and that because that's the way we saw our grandparents do it. You see the question is... do we feel it like our grandparents felt it. And if we don't – STOP says the Lord our God. Thank you Holy Spirit, cause somebody got that.

It's time now to *stop* pretending and get genuine for Christ (the one who <u>didn't</u> pretend to die for us but genuinely gave up his life for us). It's time now to accept the truth about ourselves so that we can be healed. My brothers and sisters if nothing else, we need to *stop* and break the chain of pretending, and *stop* wondering what others are going to say about us. To be honest, sometimes (more than not) people are just waiting for you to say something about Christ, then they just join right in (so happy that you were bold enough to say something first). An you know something else, sometimes it helps them to be bold the next time their in a conversation. It's like a domino affect and if we're going to start a chain, lets start this one... STEP OUT ON FAITH. We need to *stop* and listen for the voice of God.

FATHER GOD, HELP US RIGHT NOW TO
LISTEN FOR, HEAR, AND OBEY YOU. AMEN.

Notes

Notes

CHAPTER TWO

Sometime ago the media began reporting senseless violence in our public schools, being committed by the youth themselves.

I arose one morning to yet another horrific incident. I prayed, "Dear Father, I come before you now (your daughter) praying earnestly for something that I can do or say to someone to help the children understand, this is **definitely no**t the way." If the children are our future and they're carrying around this much... anger, hatred, animosity, fear, confusion and negativity in their hearts, without a change - we're doomed! My heart was so heavy at that moment I cried out, "There's got to be a way to save the children from such destructive attitudes and behaviors...

Oh Lord! I pray that you would save our children around the world from this mass destruction that satan has **entrapped** in their minds to kill, steal, and destroy everything and everybody (including themselves) which is good."

That very day (during my lunch break) God gave me this poem, entitled... **Try The Son Instead of The Gun**

When you hurt deep
The pain does seep
Into the mind evil thoughts sometimes leap
You must resist the evil urge to act
It's only satan and that's a fact
He continues to come to steal, kill, and destroy
Hoping to "No Doubt" rob you of your joy
But there's a Savior, Jesus is his name
He'll give you back your life, your soul no longer lame
He'll give you that joy you so desperately seek
And for the first time ever, you'll feel truly meek

This was my way of expressing the emotions that I was feeling and letting go or emptying out the pain that had become stored in the depth of my heart and the fore-front of my mind. God indeed, did a new thing. He took the words that he had given me that day and published it (Book: Dreams and Fantasies) also posted it online (poetry.com) so it would be available for all. I'm a living witness that God can and will use anybody, at anytime for His glory (if we allow ourselves to be used).

Hopefully, this will help encourage the young people and adults alike...***take the time to <u>think</u> (Godly) before acting***.

"THINK"… (Godly thoughts)

Satan is counting on us not to think - this is how he uses us. If we did (take the time to think *first*) he would (satan) lose his power to control us and therefore, we would not carry out his sinister deeds. James 4:7 states *"Submit yourselves, then, to God. Resist the devil and he will flee from you" (NIV).* Satan will only flee momentarily. Never forget that the flesh and the spirit are always at war and that the flesh will never be completely eradicated until death (of the flesh) do them part. Romans 8:6 says, *"The mind <u>set</u> on the flesh is death, but the mind <u>controlled</u> by the Spirit is life and peace" (NIV)* How do you resist the devil, by taking the time of THINK? Now, lets take a look at some definitions of "*<u>Think</u>*."

- To have or *formulate in the mind*
- To reason about or reflect on; *ponder*
- To judge or regard; *look upon*
- To believe; *suppose*
- To except; *hope*
- To remember; *call to mind*
- To visualize; *image*
- To *concentrate one's thought on*

Now, remember in everything there is…

❖ Good or Evil
❖ Right or Wrong

The Master says there is <u>no</u> in between "lukewarm." In Revelations 3:16 God says… ***"So, because you are lukewarm -neither hot nor cold - I'm about to spit you out of my mouth"*** *(NIV).* An old cliché also comes to mind "Either you're part of the problem or part of the solution. You must get this my sisters and brothers, you cannot be a little this or a little that (just like you can't be a little pregnant). Now you're probably saying, "well, we all fall down sometimes" and you would be absolutely correct. But don't fool yourselves… there is a difference between falling-down and stepping-in to "sin". We are all guilty of both, falling-down (unconsciously walking into… blinded by satan's false beauty – a mistake); stepping-in (consciously walking into… allowing satan to use us - blatantly). The Word of God tells us in Roman 3:23… ***"For all have sinned*** (past tense) ***and <u>fall</u>*** (present tense) ***<u>short</u> of the glory of God"*** *(NIV).* This is why it is imperative that we think before acting. Love yourself enough to think first.

The Word of God tells us that "Love" is the key, I Corinthians 13:3… *"If I give all I possess to the poor and surrender my body to the flames, but have not "love", I gain nothing" (NIV).*

Well, we will discuss "Love" more fully at a later time. But for right now lets stay focused. Remember…satan **cannot** control us if we first, STOP! - Take the time to "THINK" because when we do, we remember the **3Fs** (**Faithful**, **Fervent**, and **Focus…** This is why we must KEEP OUR MINDS ON **JESUS**). Hallelujah to the Lamb of God! My soul cries out… God is so *truly* awesome, and worthy of all our praise.

The Lord, our God created us with free will (the ability to choose). He first gave unto us a *mind* to aid us in making decisions: recalling past events; looking at the present; dreaming of the future; and allowing our minds to take us to a place where we ponder… If I *would of, should of,* or *could of.* This state of mind is how we deprive at our next move. We as Christians, must ask the Master to enter into this state of mind with us (whenever we elect to use our "free will" which is all the time, that's why we must… KEEP OUR MINDS ON **JESUS**). If we allow him to join us in the process of thinking, we will be victorious. Remember… satan will flee (momentarily) when God is asked to come in, giving us time to think clearly.

Use the mind that God gave us. Open our heart to be receptive. Receive his message. Listen closely with our faith filled ears. Secure our thoughts by praying over them constantly. Implement our chose while holding on to God's unchanging hands (now let me reiterate… God unchanging hands, not our brothers, daughters, mothers, spouses but God's unchanging hands. See God is the only one with unchanging hands.

We must not let the flesh control us; rather we must be lead by the spirit. Isaiah 55:8 states… *"For my thought are not your thoughts and my ways are not your ways declares the Lord" (NIV)* and Galatians 5:16 states… *So I say, live by the spirit, and you will not gratify the desires of the sinful nature (NIV).* If we stay on the path that the Master has laid out for us, we can be victorious. I read a phase somewhere once that said, "The Holy Spirit is always present to transform the desires ignited by the flesh (remember… the spirit lives in you). This does not mean, however, that the believer cannot go astray. Rather, it means that the <u>believer</u> is not doomed to do <u>battle</u> with the <u>flesh</u> in his or her <u>own</u> <u>strength</u>. Remember, the <u>battle</u> is not ours - it's the <u>Lord's</u> and I can do <u>all</u> <u>things</u> through <u>Christ</u> <u>Jesus</u> who <u>strengthens</u> <u>me</u> (did we get that... the strength (which is the Master) lives inside us. See because the Spirit is present to both <u>lead</u> and <u>empower</u>, as the believer choose to keep walking in the Spirit." Now you see how much more effective taking the time to think and letting the Master move us instead of using our own carnal (detrimental) thinking.

We allow satan to become powerful enough to over take our flesh and surpress our spirit. How you say, when we continue to focus on the desires that he places in our minds. Ezekiel 38: 10 says, ***"This is what the Sovereign Lord says: On that day thoughts will come into your mind and you will devise an evil scheme"*** *(NIV).* <u>Do not</u> ponder (meditate) on the evil desires because they will eventually cause you to **ACT**." Now you may ask "what makes her an expert (?)" Well, this is how I can explain it so explicitly, because it happened to me, I lived it. But it also shows how caring and merciful God is to us. You see, satan meant it for my bad but the Master used it for my (our) good. I committed a sin that day but the Master flipped the script and used it to show me how satan becomes powerful enough to over take us. We give him the power, stepping in to (the <u>longer</u> you ponder… the <u>stronger</u> satan becomes - Remember what ever you feed the most will become the strongest) which is ultimately the sin itself… **ACTION**. Matthew 6:24 ***"no one can serve two masters. Either he will hate the one and love the other, or he will be devoted to the one and despise the other.***

The next day while still thanking the Master for his forgiveness and mercy, I was still questioning myself "How, I (me) a christian, a women of faith, a daughter of the Most High could have betrayed the Master this way. Then, the Holy Spirit explained it to me just as I have explained it to you. You are not Jehovah God… you are flesh **but** because you have given your life to Christ, he now lives inside you beyond flesh inside your very soul and now you can resist the devil by keeping your mind focused on the righteousness of God. Now when you do ponder to long on the evil desires of satan (and it will happened remember God said ***"all have sinned and <u>fall</u> short…"***) and satan momentarily over takes you, ask the Master's forgiveness immediately (by **repenting** … honestly sorry and transforming to change by renewing your mind). It is written in Act

8:22 *"Repent of this wickedness and pray to the Lord. Perhaps he will forgive you for having such a thought in your heart."* Please get this my brothers and sisters, the thought did not start in our **heart**, it started in our **mind** and worked (our meditating on it) down to our heart. Matthew 15:9 says, *"For from within, out of men's heart, come evil thoughts, sexual immorality* (action)*, theft* (action)*, murder* (action)*, adultery* (action)*, and so on."* See how this work, evil thoughts enter the mind (satan plants); travels down to the heart (we ponder); and comes out in action (sin)... plain and simple. The Father loves us, and wants us and wants us to be part of his kingdom, all he ask of us is that we obey him... plain and simple. I didn't say easy (effortless) nor quick (fast) but plain (direct) and simple (clear). May the Father richly bless us all.

After the Holy Spirit made all of this quite clear to me he said, "Write it down and tell the world. In a more modern day language... Your mission, (don't forget the free will) if you <u>choose</u> to except it - spread the word. You see, lessons learned aren't just for one person – they're for everyone. It's called... **witnessing.**

Somewhere once I read or heard this formula, One way for believers to tell who's leading us...

God influences, confirms, and waits for us to decide (free will), satan influences, urges, and pushing us to decide (confusion).

THANK YOU GOD FOR YOUR GUIDANCE AND GRACE THAT IS NEW EVERY MORNING. AMEN

Gloria Waters

Notes

Notes

CHAPTER THREE

Well now, here we are at a very vital part in our understanding of being obedient

As we learned in the second chapter, *we need to think*. What is the first thing we do when we recognize that we've messed up; gone too far; lost our way; need a new start; or just simply "need to change?" Now, I'm going to try to articulate the meaning of all this as simple as I possibly can. But please keep in my that we are all individuals and because of that fact, we may not all comprehend the same meaning and that's alright because the Master said in his word, Isaiah 55: 11 ***"So shall my word be that goeth forth out of my mouth: it shall not return unto me void, but it shall <u>accomplish</u> that which <u>I please</u>, and it shall prosper in the thing whereto <u>I sent it</u>"*** *(KJV)*. See even God said, "everything isn't for everybody" in the same way. Let us pray. Lord give us the strength and openness to hear from you. I pray right now that you would help us Holy Spirit to tear down the strongholds that satan will attempt to place in the pathways of our minds. Please, let your words flow through this vessel so that we all will understand collectively and individually that which is meant for us while remembering your words John 7:16-17... ***So Jesus answered them and said, "My teaching is not Mine, but His who sent me. If anyone is willing to do His will, he will know of the teaching, whether it is of God or whether I speak from Myself"*** *(NASB)* Amen.

Alright, let's do this... Somewhere down the line we just - Stopped! Now, I'm not going to go into a long drawn out thing about stop because stop is self explanatory (and we've already learned about that in chapter one). So, first we *stop* (be still, no movement); then we can *think* (recall - how good God has been, concentrate on - how great God is) But the question now is how do we actually change? Well, in order to change we must *stand* and let God... remember, we must wait and be led by the Spirit and not by ourselves. Not using our own carnal minds to lead us into yet another trap but listen for Gods voice; focus on what He says; watch for His confirmation; and then... move on His command. Now I hope you didn't miss that process my brothers and sisters (wait, listen, focus, watch, and then move), you see... being led by the Spirit is a process. Just getting up and moving is what we've done all along, that's what has landed us in the stuff we're in now. And, stuff isn't always so easy to get rid of (some of us right now are still trying to get out of some stuff that we picked up 20 years ago. But you see, if we had <u>stopped</u> <u>trying</u> all those years and given it to the Master… that same stuff could have been illuminated 20 years ago). Okay, let's just get right into understanding ***stand***.

"STAND"… (And Let God)

If you recall in the introduction it stated that we need to "be still", stop trying to do it, fix it, and/or work it out. God said He would do that. Remember Exodus 14:13 ***"And Moses said unto the people, Fear ye not, <u>stand still and see the salvation of the Lord</u> which He will show you today: for the Egyptians whom ye have seen today, ye shall see them again no more ever" (KJV)***. Now who would have thought that the Red Sea would open and lay to each side so that the Israelites could pass through to get to the other side and then come together again precisely at the same time that Pharaoh's entire army attempted to pass through. Good God from Zion! How can we not honor, bless and most of all obey a master (no) "The Master" with this incredibly awesome power. You see, God is always there waiting, watching, listening, guiding, providing, changing, and simply acting on our behalf.

You ask then, where was God on September 11, 2001? He was where He always is, with all of us. How do you account for the fact that we're still here (and sane, if there is such a thing). After such an horrific ordeal to our entire nation, we're not some place twiddling our thumbs, babbling our lips, or just starring into space. It seems that everyone knew someone who knew someone who had family, friends or associates in one of those towers. See when we realize there's know way out; know one can help us; we can't do anything to help ourselves - when we truly recognize, we need to savior, a fixer, a provider, a way maker, we need a miracle worker…We Need Jesus Christ. You see that's why, when out of the blue some devastating incident happens instinctively we say, "Oh! My God" or just simply "Jesus." Because your inner man (your spirit) knows that only the creator of everything can fix anything. Yes! God can and will handle His business.

So, where was God on September 11, 2001. He was with the mother *standing* and waiting by the phone, hoping her son would call; He was with the father *standing* watching TV hoping to see a glimpse of his daughter flash on the screen; He was with those grandparents *standing* praying for the safety of their grandchild; He was with the husband *standing* pacing back and forth because he hadn't heard anything from his wife, who worked on the 102 floor of the first tower; He was with the wife *standing* frozen in her tracks because her husband just called and said, "I'm on the plane that's been hijacked, wanted to say I love you for maybe the last time." Our Father was also with the children *standing* around wondering why mummy or daddy hadn't come home. Our Father was with the Firefighter that was *standing* trying to not be overtaken by smoke. Our Father was with the Doctor who was standing over his patient desperately trying to hold on to his/her life.

Have you ever wondered why we stand up when a tragedy happens. It seems virtually impossible to sit down. That's because in battle we are to *stand*. You see, heaven is above and we must be vertical to reach our highest (remember we're soldiers in God's army... we stretch out our arms and hands toward heaven which cometh our help because our help cometh from the Lord), and when we're going through - that's exactly what's happening, "a battle." So in essence by our body language (standing) we're telling satan, "I'm <u>standing</u> upright on the side of Jesus the Christ "the Almighty" whom shall I fear in this battle, if I were to die I would still be better off than anything you could ever offer. Yeah, see we're driven by our inner man (our soul) not our outer man (our flesh). The inner man instinctively knows that something is out of sync (a storm is coming) and it instructs us through body language…no slouching, no bending, **GET INTO POSITION**. That's why the word of God says… ***"Therefore be ye also ready: for in such an hour as ye think not the Son of man cometh"*** *(KJV)*. Not only do we have to be ready for the return of the Master to come an judge the world but we also have to be ready so that the Master can use us while we're in the world. We say, "Use me Lord, I'm ready, but the questions is… are we <u>really</u> <u>ready</u> when the Lord calls us. That is the question and this is one of those questions were we need a <u>real</u> answer not yet another <u>fantasy</u> answer. You see, this is one of those times were you need to know that you know, that you know. Oh! Thank you Holy Spirit for speaking into my heart.

Let me clarify something before we go any further, notice I didn't say we needed to <u>be prefect</u>, I said we needed to <u>be ready</u>. See, *human beings* are not prefect, only the *Supreme being* is perfect, but there are instances when God need somebody… that he can use immediately. Of course, everyone isn't always ready but if we're all working toward the Kingdom, somebody should be already ready. When God calls, at least one of us should be able to *stand* with a glide in our stride, READY to head'em up and move'em out – with some pep in our step, READY to *stand* tall and firm for Christ and a dip in our hip READY for satan to bring it on. See we have to let satan know… though you come to throw strongholds into my life, I will stand on the side of righteousness, I will not waver, Oh! No, I will not be moved . Do you remember I Corinthians 12: 25… ***"That there should be no schism in the body; but that the members should have the same care one for another"*** *(KJV.)* This is talking about spiritual gifts - no part of the body is more important than another. See that's the same with people, no one person is more important than another. God made no one person better than another, remember Romans 2:11… ***For God does not show favoritism"*** *(NIV).* But because we are all our own individual person, none of us do everything exact alike or at the exact same time (unless of course, we have rehearsed it for some time) but that's not the norm. Everybody isn't always ready but definitely somebody should be ready. Lord God I ask you, if I have not made clear to your people what it is that you would have for them to understand, that you would fix it in their hearts and minds so that they may be blessed. Help us heavenly Father and we thank you right now for your grace and your mercy.

41

Now that we have a better understanding of when, how, where and why we *stand*, let's now look at the dictionary's definitions of stand...

> ## to take an upright position
> **Remember this...** *So in essence by our body language (standing) we're telling satan, "I'm standing upright on the side of Jesus the Christ "The Almighty"*

> ## to maintain an erect position
> **Remember this...***The inner man instinctively knows that something is out of sync (a storm is coming) and it instructs us through body language...no slouching, no bending, GET INTO POSITION.*

> ## to grow in a vertical direction
> **Remember this...***You see, heaven is above and we must be vertical to reach our highest*

Now personally, my summary for *stand*...is to be sincere. You must be sincere in the eye sight of God (remember... he looks at your heart). Once again I didn't say perfect but sincere...sincere about the one who's sincere about you. See it's imperative that we learn to *stand* and wait until God commands us to move. You see, when we ask the Father to act on our behalf, we can't rush him – we must wait on

<u>him</u>. Sometimes we think God is taking too long so we began to move without his permission. Do you remember what happen to King Saul in I Samuel 13: 13-14 it states **"You acted foolishly," Samuel said. "You have not kept the command the Lord your God gave you; if you had, he would have established your kingdom over Israel for <u>all time</u>. But now your kingdom will not endure; the Lord has sought out a man after his own heart and appointed him leader of his people, because you have not kept the Lord's commands."** *(NIV)* Now, listen to me closely… All though we can't see it, God has a plan but according to the decisions <u>we've made</u> in our own lives <u>determines</u> where and how God <u>directs us</u> in order for us to <u>receive</u> that which <u>we have asked</u> of him. See now, maybe that was just a little too deep, well… let's just break it down. If we hadn't <u>messed it up</u>, God wouldn't have had to <u>clean it up</u> and therefore we would have received it <u>sooner</u> and enjoyed it <u>longer</u>. My brothers and sisters we have to start taking ownership and responsibility for our own mess ups. I pray right now Lord God that you would help us to use our free will to do your will so that we can become… less of a mess.

Now in Conclusion…Choosing our own self-will over God's command is a seriously dangerous move. You see, when we reject God's plan, we allow… satan to come in (and we all know his mission statement… sole purpose of his being is to steal, kill and destroy everything which is good). Now, you know what we <u>should</u> say to that….DELETE.

THANK YOU HEAVENLY FATHER AND ALL THESE THINGS WE SAY IN JESUS NAME…AMEN.

The Love of My Life Swept Me Off My Feet THE GREAT I AM

Notes

Notes

PART TWO

Gloria Waters

FOOD FOR THOUGHT

I.   Have you ever really thought about what we're doing when we obey satan instead of God?

We <u>Betray</u> God…"We are TRADERS"

In the world today if you're labeled a "Trader," everyone, everywhere you go look at you with angry and stand at a distance as if you were contagious or something.

But isn't it wonderful and awesome to know that in the spirit world… GOD (even after we've taken the side of the evil one) still loves us and will grant us his grace, mercy, and forgiveness if we're genuinely sorry and <u>ask</u> for forgiveness.

Picture this (visualization)…
A dual – satan on the left and God on the right and you are the pond. Games over and you've chosen satan's way.
Satan starts laughing hysterically at God; he began to hold his stomach because it aches of joy of defeating God; the wells of his eyes began to fill up

and overflow with tears of sheer gladness; pointing his fingers at God; barely able to utter the words… "I told you so!"

Then you look to your right, there's God… head hung low; hands covering his face; his hands began to fill up with tears of sadness; he begins to remove his hands from his face and sees the imprint of where the nails were driven through his hands (**for you**); at that very moment he recalls a time when his body hung high on a cross as water and blood ran out of his side (**for you**).
As he looks toward you with tears streaming down his face, you feel the love that he has for you in your heart. At that very moment your eyes are opened and you recognize the players; you fall to your knees and ask God to forgive you; he smiles and say, "Your sins are forgiven."

You See… Satan Won The Battle But <u>Not The War</u>.

➢ *GOD IS NOT SO MUCH CONCERNED WITH YOUR PAST* (WHERE YOU WERE) *BUT YOUR FUTURE* (WHERE WILL YOU BE).

SOMETHING TO REMEMBER:

The PRESENT is relative – IT IS JUST A MEMORY OF A MOMENT AGO *OR* A DREAM OF A MOMENT TO COME.

SCRIPTURE…

Jesus foretells his betrayal
John 13: 21… **When Jesus had thus said he was troubled in spirit, and testified, and said, Verily, verily, I say unto you, that one of you shall betray me. (KJV)**

THINK ABOUT THIS…

We all have betrayed the Master at some point in time.
When was the last time you were Judas Iscariot?
And, have you asked for forgiveness?
*Let Go and Let God… **Heal you!!!***

FOOD FOR THOUGHT

II. Have you ever thought about why it's so hard to just get up when we fall, even after we've asked for forgiveness and God has grant it.

That's Satan Telling Us**... "Feel Guilty And Stay Down," Not God!... GOD WANTS US TO GET <u>FREE</u>!**

If you didn't know, now you know "satan also has a plan." He does not step off or away from us just because God has delivered us or forgave us, he just re-groups and takes a different approach at that very same situation. Remember... satan is not going to attack us on a low priority situation (satan is playing for keeps).

Brothers and sisters, when dealing with what the flesh is familiar with (use to) we have to continually get back up until doing it God's way becomes the familiar (or use to) way.

Picture this (visualization)...

A baby crawls; pulls itself up (time and time again) and continually repeats this act until walking becomes the familiar (or use to) way. During this trial and error period there's plenty of bumps and bruises, good days and bad days, disappointments and accomplishments, and finally after a journey of ups and downs the reward full-time, all the time **WALKING**.

You See… That's What <u>Saved</u> means… Freed From The <u>Old And Outdated</u> And Rewarded With The <u>New And Improved</u> **ALL THE TIME**.

➤ **GOD WANTS US TO KNOW THAT WE DON'T HAVE TO STAY TRAPPED IN BONDAGE** (ALWAYS FEELING THAT THERE'S SOMETHING MISSING BUT NEVER KNOWING OR BEING TOO AFRAID TO FIND OUT WHAT) **THAT FEELING IS GOD CALLING… "THERE IS JOY AND PEACE WAITING FOR YOU."**

SOMETHING TO REMEMBER:
Satan wins **ONLY**… when you give up
GET UP!!!

SCRIPTURE…

Gloria Waters

A righteous man falls but rises again
Proverbs 24:16... **for though a righteous man falls seven times, he rises again, but the wicked are brought down by calamity.**

THINK ABOUT THIS...

Satan has many weapons in his arsenal (sickness, hatred, lust, envy, malice, etc.), but never give in to satan's most powerful weapon "discouragement." If he can trap you deep and long enough in discouragement (which is his actual goal) were as to **stop** the communication between you and God... BINGO - games over, satan's scores. (Don't forget... this is the game of life and satan plays for keeps).

At this point he has already stolen your joy; killed you hopes; and now ready to destroy you "death."

My brothers and sisters we must never forget the difference between a righteous man (continuous communication with God) and a wicked man (no communication with God).

Feeling guilty (discouragement) is satan's way...
*Let Go and Let God... **Heal you!!!***

54

FOOD FOR THOUGHT

III. Now, think about the first two thoughts… obeying satan instead of God and so hard to get up when we fall.

These are the two major things that happened to Judas Iscariot. Obeying satan…

- ➢ took a little money here, took a little money there
- ➢ The more he took the more he needed
- ➢ Found a new way to get money even quicker
- ➢ betraying a friend
- ➢ causes trouble in the lives of others
- ➢ bringing fear and hurt throughout the land
- ➢ but most of all; turning the Master over to the enemy

Judas eventually became so discouraged (satan's strongest weapon) with himself he killed himself (would not allow himself to forgive himself).

Who will you allow to become the stronger influence in your mind?

Picture this (visualization)...

You're a kid, at home all alone and decide you'll look at some television. What's on...

- Series - (Everwood, Alias, etc.) how to cry your eyes out and be depressed all the time
- Reality Shows – (The Bachelorette, Joe Millionaire, Mole, etc.) how to humiliate others
- Excitement - (Craft, Buffy, Angel, etc.) how to fight, love, and hate demons
- Comedy - (Girlfriends, Grace, etc.) gays, sex, lies, and call people out of there names in one easy step
- News - tragedy... the worse the better, and if it's not bad...the media will make it sound bad

So much for that, lets play some video games...

- How to kill a pedestrian in 9 seconds
- Blow open the chest of a cop
- Run over a baby in a stroller

Boring, lets see what's around the house…

- Dad's gun
- Mama's drugs
- Big brother's magazines

From a kid to an adult… without intervention of a different life, this will surely lead to… Death!
You Can Change…Choice Life

SOMETHING TO REMEMBER:

We're always talking about I'll be <u>glad</u> when (the kids grow up, the bills are paid off, etc.) stop waiting…
BE <u>GLAD</u> <u>NOW</u>.

SCRIPTURE…

Judas kills himself
Matthew 26:3-5… **Then Judas, which had betrayed him, when he saw that he was condemned, repented himself, an brought again the thirty pieces of sliver to the chief priests and elders saying, "I have sinned in that I have betrayed the innocent blood. And they said, "What is that to us? See thou to that. And he cast down the pieces, of silver in the temple and departed, and went and hanged himself.**

THINK ABOUT THIS…

See, satan is <u>physically</u> asking you, "how low and how long can you go" and he will continue taunting you (as long as you allow him to, by not getting up and trying again,…forgiving yourself) until he has you right were he wants you…**crippled**. Then he'll wipe you out and while you're dying he'll be laughing in your face saying, "one down, many to go." Bye, Bye.

God allows you to go through stuff to bring you into a closer relationship with him... not to push you away from him. But the choice is yours whether to come closer to him or back way. I say again my brothers and sisters... **CHOICE LIFE**.

Two strangers stranded on an island. Do they continue to be strangers or do they get to know one another? And is it likely that they will forget each other once they're rescued?
*Let Go and Let God... **Heal you!!!***

Gloria Waters

*ABOUT
THE
WRITER*

Gloria Waters

Biography

In reference to my Christian walk, where do I start? Well, I guess at the beginning. Like many Christians (some for a short time and others for a lifetime) I confessed my sins and believed that Jesus Christ is Lord. Afterwards, I attended church regularly on Sunday mornings; put a few dollars in my tithing envelopes; occasionally attended Wednesday night bible study; always had a bible in the house but mainly only read it during church services; prayed to God to do this or that for me and thanked him when it was manifested in my life (but mostly prayed heartfelt prayers when there was some sort of strategy and/or turmoil going on). Oh! I thought I had it going on. I gave clothes to the goodwill; put change in the salvation army kettle; donated can goods for baskets; gave money when the pastor announced there were families in need; and so on. <u>I was a good christian woman</u> (so I truly thought).

You see my brothers and sisters, back in the day when I was coming up the Preachers preached the word. See if this sound sort of the way it was at your church. Time for the sermon:

First - the reading of the scripture
Second - brief meaning of the scripture
Third - a life experience of the scripture (a story of some sort)
Fourth - religious excitement – worship (Grand finale)
Fifth - altar call (conversion)

Hardly anyone attended the bible study back in the day. So most of us really didn't understand what being <u>saved</u> meant. And when you asked people who had been saved for a while questions, they would say something like "Don't drink liquor, smoke cigarettes, pray and obey the Ten Commandments. See because most of us back then were not readers of the word (for various reason), we just followed the advise of the elders and followed what we saw them do (and I'm telling you… lots of times what they said to do and what you saw them do… didn't match up). These very situations are some of the reasons that many people today won't even try to find out what **God** is all about. But I come to tell you today my brothers and sisters, don't get it twisted, ***"God is not religion (a tradition) - God is God (the Spirit) all by himself."***

Take the time to get to know God for yourself – by reading the word and asking him to show you the way (he will you know). Paul said in II Timothy 2:15 (KJV) ***"Study to show thyself approved unto God, a good workman that needeth not be ashamed, rightly dividing the word of truth."*** and II Timothy 2:15 (Book) states, ***"Work hard so God can approve you. Be a good worker, one who does not need to be ashamed and who correctly explains the word of truth."*** II Timothy 2:14-26 is a exhortation of very sound doctrine (a warning of very sound principles). See, this is how some have led others to believe things that weren't exactly the truth, because they speak with unfamiliar tongues. Unfamiliar tongues… what is that? You see mixing words; using large words, and/or been unable to understand ones speech can land you in big trouble. I think I said this before earlier in the book, don't believe that old cliché because "what you don't know - can hurt you." Please, stop letting others tell you what God can do for you… find out for yourself. The Master said we must witness to our brothers and sisters about what he has <u>done</u> for us, so that you will know that he <u>can</u> and <u>will</u> do the same for you (remember… God has no favorite person). Now in keeping in the will of God, I would like to tell you of a few wonderful eye and heart opening experiences (revelations from God) I have ever encountered. Thank you Holy Spirit. First, Jesus Christ died on the cross so that we <u>all</u> could have the right to be apart of Gods kingdom (if we choose to do so). He willingly gave up his life as a one time ransom payment for <u>all</u> our lives. How could that be? He was the Son of God (without sin) that's why only his life (a pure soul) could pay once for all times. Jesus knew what his mission was when he came. He knew he was the… **"Way Maker."** This is why even before he died he told his disciples and his followers ***"Whosoever will come after me, let him deny himself and take up his cross and follow me"*** *(KJV)*. Now, I reminded you of all that to bring to mind this point… **this is your chose.** The Master urged us to choose life (Deuteronomy 30:11-20). Jesus told us a story of a king who prepared a great wedding feast for his son that illustrates the way into the kingdom of heaven and how he wants to share it with us (but we must come correctly), Matthew 22:16 ***"For many are called, but few are chosen."*** *(Book)*

I wanted to refresh your memory of all these things to say… As Luther Barnes once said, **"It's a mighty good thing to be chosen by God."** But in order to be chosen we must show ourselves approved with a longing, hungering, and thirst for God. Searching all the time for more and more of how to please him; do his will; and be more like him. When you truly cry out to God sincerely with a urging to get to know him (nothing else, just him), he will send you a revelation that will sweep you off your feet. You know many people ask me why is it that most of the time I reference God as <u>Master</u>? The answer is quite clear… I am his slave (having a willingness to <u>serve</u> him always). Some African American's have a problem with the word "slave" and "Master" but that does not concern me because everyone is a slave to something (think about), and I can't think of anything or anybody else I'd rather be a slave to… than God (**Romans 6:19-23** - you'll find confirmation of this). Well, let us return our focus back to the issue at hand. God wants us to truly understand the meaning of life and him (which is actually all the same). Maybe my life experiences can help you do just that. Thank you Almighty Father. You see, I have a habit of journalizing meaningful life experiences and I'm going to share them with you… just as I recorded them.

So hang on as I recall and you travel along - as we venture into a journey that seems so long ago.

Holy Master, I pray that your people will
allow these life lessons to do for them
what they did for me. Open eyes that
could not see (II Kings 6:17).

To bring you up to speed, let me highlight prior incidents that lead up to this enlightenment. I had prayed for the Lord to deliver me from smoking cigarettes (because I had allowed satan to use this, and he was using it as an instrument to kill me (don't front - call it what it is). See some things in our lives we have allowed to become so strong (an addiction) until now they control us, instead of us controlling them). Seems like I tried a million times and just couldn't quit. A couple weeks prior, God had answered my pray and I was excited. After a few days I started having these thoughts of how it would taste if I tried a cigarette (remember…I had smoked for 20 years – how dumb was that). Seems like every time I turned around I was having that thought. Then I thought, "It couldn't hurt, just one cigarette. Finally, one day I bummed one from somebody, initially it made me dizzy but after a couple of drags I was O.K. The next day I bummed another until I eventually bought a pack. I was hooked again. I was upset that I had been so weak and allowed myself to be suckered in so easily. I pray to the Master to forgive me but <u>I</u> <u>could</u> <u>not</u>

<u>forgive</u> <u>myself</u>. The guilt of betraying the Master and returning to the one thing that I had so desperately prayed that he would deliver me from was eating me up. That evening prior to going out, I was suppose to be watching the game but my mind was so consumed with begging for forgiveness and crying out to God to help me once more. Somehow though it was different, I was seeking the Lord like I had never done before. I talked to him straight up like I would a person standing directly in front of me (that was the first time I had every truly been so direct with the Master); I asked him did he hear me; I told him that I needed him to talked to me, talk to me so that I could understand him (like I'd heard others say that he'd talked to them); I told him that I didn't want someone else to tell me Jesus told me to tell you. I wanted to know that I know that I know without a shadow of a doubt; give me a sign (I wanted a sign that I would know definitely that it was him and not just a coincidence). I was getting hyped y'all, I went as for as to say even if you have to put me on a bed of affliction to show and deliver me once more. Oops! My brothers and sisters remember these words... Proverbs 4:7 ***"Wisdom is the principal thing; therefore get wisdom and with***

all thy getting get understanding."*(KJV). Amen. Amen. Amen.*

When I Slipped Into The Light...

Sitting in the middle of my bed one night, suddenly I had a taste for a Big Mac. You know, that all beef patty, special sauce, lettuce, cheese, pickles,... well, you know. Huh! I thought, half time is about to start (watching the VT verse Florida State game, checking out my boy Michael Vick and "yes" some women do like football). Boy, do I have great timing or what? I decided... I'll just slip on a pair of sweat pants, tuck my night gown inside, throw on my jacket, zip it up and no one would ever be the wiser (or so I thought). Just going throw the drive-thru, threre isn't even any reason to carry my purse. So, I'll just take a few dollars since the big Mac was on special (2 for $2.00), besides I already had a 2 littler Pepsi in the frig.

As I walked out onto the porch and looked around this feeling came over me, felt sort of cryptic. I shoved the feeling but as I exited the driveway and started down the street I thought, how absolutely quiet and still it seemed. As I turn toward the highway and started up the ramp it was like everything had stopped, like time had just stood still. Then as I approached the stop sign, I looked all around me and nothing way moving anywhere. No cars on the street; no leaves waving on the trees; no crickets chirping in the brushes; no sound anywhere. As I pulled out onto the highway, suddenly there was a small black sports car rushing out of control, screeching across the grassy median headed straight for me. There was no time to say or do anything. I heard a voice say, "Keep you foot on the brake. By the time I said Oh! He hit me. I closed my eyes and prayed to the Master to forgive my sins as my vehicle spun round and around, out of control. Suddenly, something hit the back of my car and it started to spin in the opposite direction of before. Trust me, it's definitely true what they say about your entire life flash in front of you. To me it was like flash cards of different but memorable episodes of my life, from the beginning of childhood straight through to that present moment. I remember thinking... it must be my time because my life is flashing in front of me, while at the same time thinking... It seems like a long time has past but somehow knowing it had only been minutes. I also remember saying to myself, "I don't believe I'm still conscience."

Finally my car stopped. Immediately I noticed it was extremely hard for me to breathe and my body was so drained of every oz. of energy, I couldn't move. I thought to myself, "If I could only release the seatbelt maybe I could breathe a little better. Unfortunately, my arms felt so heavy I couldn't move them. Maybe I could mustard up enough energy to pull the door handle and the seatbelt would release automatically. Once again I called on the Master to give me that strength... I so desperately needed at that moment. The door handle was approximately 6 to 8 inches away but my arm felt like lead. Finally my arm slowly begin to lift and I stretched out my fingers so to rest on the door handle (thanks be to God that I had the type of handle that didn't require a lot of effort to pull). I slightly pulled the handle and the door slung open and the belt released me. But to my surprise I felt no relief, it still felt like I had a concrete slab laying in my chest.

At that moment my condition worsened. I didn't know what was wrong, why couldn't I breathe? I began to panic (which didn't help matters at all). At that point I realized this was not going to be just a ER visit and then home with some pain medication...THIS WAS GOING TO BE SOMETHING SERIOUS.

Suddenly I saw a guy running toward me with a bloody face and a frantic voice yelling, "Are you alright?' In a low whispering voice I answered,

"No, I'm not. Then, in a anxious and panic voice he cried out... I'm going down here to try an find someone to help us. I promise I'll be right back, I'm not going to leave you.

By this time it had begun a very fine drizzle and there it was again, that nothingness in the air. No sound, no movement just stillness. As I looked on to the highway I thought, "I don't believe this is happening. Here I am sitting in my car that's turned sideways in the middle of an interstate highway (facing the direction of oncoming traffic); with the driver's door laying wide open; looking out down the highway with misty rain beating me in the face; and I can't move. I can't do anything to change this situation, I have <u>no</u> control whatsoever. I'M HELPLESS! If you ever wondered what "helpless" really feels like, just close your eyes and picture what you just read and imagine this is you. I begin to talk to God about all kinds of things, especially for saving me. As I talked to God I seemed to have forgotten were I was and instead of begin frighten I felt peaceful. But oh you know satan would find a way to sneak into the mind and try to create havoc. (You see my friends, this is why we must stay on guard all the time— enjoy our peace but still stay alert. Once we allow ourselves to become so relaxed in the basting of peace that we just let our minds go, satan comes plowing in like a bulldozer and catches us off guard and throws another fine mess in our mix. Remember we are soldiers in an army and it's O.K. to laugh, enjoy the peace and the glory of God but never forget where you are… still **in the war**. You see, I was so tired and drained until I just wanted to feel the good all over but he also knew what I wanted (satan doesn't always come fighting up front and having to battle you for entrance, sometimes he sneaks in throw our weaknesses and catches us off guard…BEWARE!).

Suddenly my mind wandered to "what if a car come speeding around the curb and don't see me in time to stop (remember… I was in the middle of the interstate). My heart started to race and at that very moment I saw a white van coming toward me. I couldn't turn my head away because I couldn't move (remember) so I quickly closed my eyes and prayed once again. With my eyes closed it seemed as though I was looking at a television screen. I saw my spirit lift up out of the earthly shell and I actually stared at the oncoming van with such concentration I've never known. The van began to slow down and when I opened my eyes a woman was briskly walking toward me crying out, "Oh! My God, can I help you. I replied, "can't move." She then asked if there was anyone she could call for me, holding her cell phone In her hand. She kneeled down beside me to hear as I slowly struggled out a number (it was to my cousin, whose apartment building was directly at the foot of the ramp). Also, at that moment I heard all sort of sirens, police, fire, ambulance, everything. It seemed like before I could even blink it was lit up like Christmas out there and people were everywhere.

Before I knew it, there were lights flashing in my eyes from every direction; people talking, yelling, screaming; and vehicle engines roaring. I just wanted it to all go away. So, I tuned it all out, I saw everything but I heard nothing. As I sat there with every oz. of energy depleted, I began to once again talk to the Master, "Lord, I know this is bad but I trust that you will (if it's your will) deliver me safely throw this tragedy. But, if this is my time, I'm ready... I only ask that you will take me quickly, please don't let me suffer in pain? You see, all my life that was my greatest fear. Growing up in S.E. Washington D.C. I had been in many different situations in my lifetime and many tight spots, then moving here to Virginia at seventeen (being wild and crazy) wasn't no picnic in the park either. But through it all I never had bodily pain that I couldn't take some medication and feel better (but I had seen many people in excruciating pain). But before it was over I would experience that very pain. See, the Master always have a plan, even if we don't always know what it is, but it will all become clear when he says it's time. *As I regained the awareness of my surroundings (all the noise) and was about to lose it, a gentleman (a fireman) kneeled down beside me and said, "Don't worry, everything is going to be O.K. Where are you hurting? I replied, "I can't breathe." Don't try to talk anymore, he said as he tried to explain the situation to the paramedic who was attempting to kneel beside us. As the fireman moved to the side the paramedic moved in a little closer to me, he tried to explain without alarming me that they were just trying to figure out the best way to get me out of the car (little did I know at that time how truly mangled the car was... front smashed to the back and the back smashed to the front). Even though I didn't know how bad things were, I could tell that it was awful by the expressions on people's faces.*

At that moment my niece (who lived in the apartments below the ramp) came running toward me crying and screaming, "Oh! My God. Moments later her mother arrived at the scene and grabbed her and held her close, while tears screamed down her face. My heart just broke into little fragments (at that moment I forgot all about me, I was hurting dreadfully because they were hurting).

Then, all of a sudden there was this quick loud bursting sound (like a car back firing), and everyone's eyes widen and they began to back away. The paramedic that was kneeling beside me looked over toward his partner who was running toward us, the one kneeling asked, "What happened." As his partner reached the car door he screamed with a timorous voice, "We have no more time, we have to get her out NOW! (the other vehicle had just burst into flames... right next to the passenger side of mine). The paramedic who had been kneeling beside me stood up and placed his hands behind my shoulders I cried out, "No...please stop, you're killing me," but he continued to pull me out while the other paramedic grabbed my legs and they laid me on the stretcher. One of them kneeled down beside me an apologized but said they had no chose as they put a neck collar around my neck. I signaled with my finger to come closer and I whispered, "I'm going to die right here if you insist that I lay straight, please, lift my head up (you see, they had laid me flat and it was taking extremely to much energy to take a breather, even a small one...energy I didn't have). Thank God for Jesus — cause I knew

I couldn't continue to struggle to breathe any longer, God just gave me a kind of calmness and from that moment on - I just went with the flow. No longer crying, trying to breathe, nothing… just calm. See my flesh couldn't go any longer… this was one of those times when God carried me. Thank you again Almighty God.

*On the way to the hospital one of the paramedics continued to talk to me. I heard him and responded but was not focusing on anything he was saying. Finally, we arrived at the hospital and as they rolled me into the ER entrance I saw a doctor coming toward me and they all were talking but it was as if the volume was being turned down. I didn't really care about that though because I was fallen into a sleep like I never felt before, I could feel myself smiling and I was thinking, "Oh! This is going to be some good sleep here, just bring it on." **This is when I slipped into the Light**. Suddenly, there was this light that seemed to consume me and then I was in a mist of clouds and this brightness. This wasn't like a bulb light or sunlight, just a brightness type of light. I turned around and saw the doctors working on me (and before you even ask… no, I didn't feel afraid), I didn't quite understand how I could be in both places at the same time but somehow I also kind of knew I wasn't in Virginia anymore (funny… I didn't feel sad about it, I actually felt sort of*

relieved). When I think about it today, I think Uh!
That must be that type <u>Rest</u> that the Master have in
store for his people. Believe me... You Don't Want
To Miss It.

The next thing I remember... I was awakening
and I heard a voice say, "Do you know, that you
know now!" Suddenly as I opened my eyes this joy
(like I never felt before) came over me so strong and
overwhelming, I wanted to get up and jump and
*shout and scream and tell the world, "**GOD SPOKE***
***TO ME**." Instead, tears just rolled down my face.*

If you noticed I said I <u>wanted</u> to do all these things. See, I realized when I awakened I was strapped to a bed; my flesh was completely exhausted (although my spirit was as high as a kite); there was tube in my nose, mouth, chest, and a few other places; I was in a neck collar that felt like it was made of lead; and people standing all around (co-workers, family and friends).

Now, the point I want to express here it that when you began to truly seek God's face and cry out to him for a closer, intimate relationship with him…you are asking for it, it's on. Satan is going to throw everything he have at you (from above, beneath, left, right, front and back), and he's going to use the very thing he know you fear the most because he want us to say (all the way from the depth of our soul) I GIVE UP, IT'S NOT WORTH ALL THIS…**STOP THIS TRAIN AND LET ME OFF**. But the Master warns us of satan's mission and of his coning tactics if we persist in following the ways of righteousness. Jesus said, (John 10:10) ***"The thief comes only to steal, kill, and destroy; but I come that you might have life and have it to the fullest."(NIV)*** Now also, do you remember Luke 4:1-13 (read it for yourself) how satan tempted Jesus (the only perfect one) with the things he knew could tempt Jesus the most. **First** - with food because he knew Jesus had not eaten anything in forty day and was hungry – *and Jesus was in the flesh at this time*; **Second** - with authority over all the earth (see, satan also knew what Jesus primary mission was here on earth) and he was offering it to him without suffering (so he exclaim) because he knew Jesus was tired and also that the time was near for Jesus to fulfill his mission - *and Jesus was in the flesh at this time*; and **Third** - with show and tell because this would not have been in the will of the Father (merely to show off - boasting) which would have been in direct violation of the Father (disobedience) – *and Jesus was in the flesh at this time*. See, satan hoped since Jesus was in the flesh he may have a chance to convince him to at least (for a moment) consider **following** him. Now, if satan was this persistent with Jesus Christ, you know… he will be on us. Pulling out all the stops. Walking about seeking whom he may devour (I Peter 5:8). Once satan sees you crying out for real for real to the Master for a closer relationship with him (wanting nothing else), Oh I say again my friends… it's on. But, oh yeah, (there's a but in here)… The Master says if we hang in there (and we can) and endure to the end… (he never said it was going to be easy, in fact, he said it would be rough and tough) the reward would be well worth all the suffering and more. Now, don't misunderstand my brothers and sisters, when I speak of suffering, I'm not speaking in the sense of in pain just because I was in an accident but in the sense of being beat up by satan. I tell people all the time, if I had to do it all again to hear the voice of God... I would. Thank God I do now have that type of relationship with the Master and I pray that I will always be this close or closer to him.

Now, before we proceed to the next testimonial (life lesson), remember earlier I warned you to never forget Proverbs 4:7 (wisdom and understanding)? I wanted you to remember that because no one warned me to be careful of what you ask for. Don't just go around saying things because that's what you've heard others say (without the understanding – God warned us to read the word daily and study it to show ourselves approved). You see, I spoke that tragedy in my own life. Not only did God hear me that night but so did satan. Once I spoke it, he was allowed to do it. But thanks be to God that he (God) also heard me begging to know (for myself), to be so close to him that I could hear him. So once again satan was trying to use my ignorance for bad but God (the Holy One) used my hunger to bring me closer. Be careful what you ask for my brothers and sisters. Thank you Almighty God!

Alright then, let's move on. I hope you also recall that previously I told you that satan don't stop once he knows you're serious, that only makes him even more determined to bring you back into his fold. I was hospitalized for a few weeks after the accident but after about a couple of weeks I began to experience this sort of tingling sensation in my right hand every time I moved it, until I couldn't even think about moving it without it sending me into excruciating pain. Of course, the doctors all thought that I was just being a wimp but my family knew something was desperately wrong. You see, they've always leaned on me for strength (I'm the strong one in the family they'd say… physically and otherwise). Before I could even recover there he was again (satan) trying to bet me down. I hope you're all getting this. This is part of his strategy…keep pounding away while we're in a weaker state of mind and body. Only a fool would wait for you to recover and trust me… satan is no fool when is comes to accomplishing his mission. He is determined to stay on point, that's why we need to be just as determined to follow the truth (**GOD**). The staff finally realized that there was something terribly wrong when they needed to run some test and I had continuously refused to move. They brought the machine to my room and I still refused to let them touch me. The doctor grabbed me to turn me over and I just lost it… I screamed to the top of my lungs (which they were also trying to recover, see one of my diagnoses was a punctured lung); my body began to shake all over; and my mind had become distorted. I heard the doctor yelling as he released me but I couldn't make out what he was saying. Finally I heard him say, "What is your name?" I answered and he cleared the room. I had cried and screamed so deep until after they left I could only lay there with tears screaming down my face. Funny, how vividly you can remember things that you would like to forget and how quickly you forget things that you would like to remember. It's also amazing to me that I would remember any of these incidents because I was in so much pain during these times. God does work in mysterious ways. The next day another doctor came to see me, she said, "I think I know what's wrong with you and I'm sorry that we didn't recognize it before but it's something that we know very little about and even less on how to treat it. I think you have nerve damage. If you would allow me to do two simple things, we will know for sure." She did warn me that one may be painful but the other (if she's right) would not. First… she grabbed my arm tightly. To my amazement, I felt no pain (O.K. I was psyched).

Next, she took a toothpick an slightly stroked my arm. Pain like I never knew filled my entire body. You know that knife cutting, sharp, quick intense pain where all you can do is tremble. Yeah, that type pain. As she stood there with her hands over her mouth, tears begin to rolled down her face as she murmured, "We're all done, you rest and we'll talk tomorrow.

So to make a long story short… I had been in a major auto accident that left with me with numerous recuperation challenges (nerve damage… which there aren't any real medication to stop the pain or help in it's regeneration and before it begins to regenerate (if it ever does) you lose <u>all</u> control of that area. This is one of those "only time can heal" processes; a broken neck (2 places); a punctured lung; cracked ribs; with lacerations and contusions). Overall summary…my entire body was totally traumatized… but my soul was overflowing with joy.

My brothers and sisters, what I'm trying to get you to realize is that… **it's true** - you can rejoice even in your pain (*but only if you have a <u>real</u> relationship with the Master in your heart*). The thorn and the third heaven that Paul speaks about (II Corinthians 12: 1-10) explains just how this is possible. The joy of the revelation on the inside is stronger than the pain of the thorn on the outside. See that's just it… it's not logical (carnal), it's supernatural (spiritual). This is why it's so hard for many to believe today. Faith is - believing in that which you cannot side with the human eye. You know, some people say that their open-minded, but in the same breathe they say, "I don't believe that." Well, What is open-minded? Having an opened mind means thinking it could be, it may be, and/or nothing is impossible (thinking outside the box; going where no one has gone before and finally… no explanation at all). So be very careful around those who say, "I'm an open-minded person" but also say, "that's not logical". The Master warns us about doubled-minded persons. You can not be an open-minded and a logical person at the same time about the same situation. Let's just get real and stop fronting.

Speaking of getting real (smile), let me <u>really</u> get back on track. You see my brothers and sisters this is one of my weaknesses, there has been so many times when the Master rescued me… I just want to tell it all in one breathe (see, I don't want to leave anything out – don't want to leave you hanging or unclear) but even now, in the mist of everything going on in my mind, I can hear the Holy Spirit speaking… "Stay focused," the Master will take care of the rest. Thank you Holy One of Israel.

There's a lesson… even in a fluke

After several weeks of recuperating at home, my doctor thought it best if I returned to work (maybe it would help take my mind off the pain). One of my co-workers lived a couple blocks away and graciously offered to pick me up in the mornings. One morning (after only two weeks) I was hurrying to the kitchen and slipped. As I was falling to the floor because I was trying to protect my injured hand, I did not think about the glass I had in the other. The glass shattered and as I started to pick myself up I noticed there was a lot of blood on the floor but I had no idea were it was coming from. I was about to rub my head (as thought to say… what now!) and I saw blood shushing out of my hand next to my thumb. Because my right hand was already inoperable, I couldn't tighten anything around my left hand. At that moment my girlfriend was ringing the doorbell but I could not get the door open because I had no hands, as blood dripped from the soaked towel I had wrapped around my hand. I was crying and screaming, "I can't get the door open" as I explained I had injured my other hand. She couldn't open the window because it was locked from the inside and I couldn't unlock it. Again, I called on the only one who could help me... "The Master." A voice gently and calmly said, "place one finger on the lock on the door knob and slightly push." I obeyed and my friend opened the door herself. God is a Mighty Good God! You see, prior to her coming that morning, I had already opened the door an taken the lock off the screen door. Having no idea (at that time) what would take place later but... **God did**. A prime example of God working it out before we even know what's happening. *To make a long story short... I had severed my thumb directly in the grove line and had also damaged the nerve (can you believe that). Remember what I told you earlier, satan is <u>always</u> busy. Never giving you time to regroup or re-coop (whatever the case maybe). Anyway, lots of things happened during this point where the Lord showed up and showed out (reminding satan and I that he was still there and in control...nothing could happen unless he allowed it). Not truly understanding all this at the time... I continually wondered why the Master was allowing me to go through this Job experience (even though I didn't know what the reason was, I did know... there was one).*

After a few weeks with virtually no use of my hands (even though the Lord was allowing me to go through some things...he was still true to his word "still my provider" see, during the last few months since the accident I had started to regain some use of a few fingers on my right hand, not a lot but at least I could pick up small items (a wash cloth, dish cloth, a sheet of paper, a napkin, and so on but still nothing with any real weight) the Dr. took the stitches out and I could once again return to work.

I had been back to work approximately three to four weeks when one day out of the blue (as I was having a business conversation with some co-workers) I suddenly could not catch my breathe. I started rapaciously trying to get air but it was as if my throat had closed. One of my co-workers brought me a glass of water and as quickly as it started it stopped. When the ambulance arrived I told them that I was O.K. but explained to them what happened and they seemed to think (maybe)the peanuts I had been eating went down the wrong way. I agreed but was still cautious and concerned about the incident (since it had never happened before and I always munched out on peanuts).

After that, periodically I would get phlegm caught in my throat and it seemed to be getting *harder and harder to get it out. At my next doctor's visit I explain the situation (by the way, all this was totally new to me... seeing doctors frequently; being sick; relying on others; believe it or not even being afraid.) So, they started running test and prescribing this and that, nothing was really working and the problem was intensifying. I had so little oxygen I would have the air conditioner turned all the way up and still felt as if I was about to spontaneously combust; sometimes in the middle of the night I would have to get up and change the sheets on my bed became they would be soaked with sweat; some mornings (when I got out of bed) I would have to stand outside in the back yard to keep from passing out; and every morning I took about an half hour just to clear some of the phlegm out of my throat before I could do anything else. I was seriously going through and not clear on why. I kept asking myself, "have I lived such a messed up life that I would be going through so long and so hard? But the truth of the matter is... the answer kept coming back "It doesn't belong to you (this life, that is). It was bought with a price along time ago. You had no <u>right</u> to mess it up (I Corinthians 6:19-20), so the answer is "yeah." This is why when I hear certain phases or songs I start to cry out to the Master...* **Thank You**! *Cause for real - you don't know my story and all that I've been through; you don't know* all the good nor bad I had to go through just to get here; and God's been so good... even though I wish I could... I can't tell it all. There is <u>no</u> words to describe the way I feel about him or the way he feels about me. HE IS MY EVERYTHING! Okay, getting back to the testimony.

I had schedule vacation for the week of July 4th and boy... I needed a break. That Monday I stay in bed until almost mid-day but when I got up, my throat was so clogged I couldn't clear it enough. I called my mother an told her what was going on with me and told her that I wanted her to go with me to the hospital and she agreed. When we arrived at the hospital they connected me to the breathing treatment machine (which the doctors had been giving me all along, along with trying other drugs and treatments for asthma, sinus, reflux, etc.). That entire week was a wash...I couldn't sleep; couldn't eat, couldn't lye down; I was in the ER everyday during this week, some days twice. The doctors in the ER (coming toward the end of the week) looked at me with such helplessness in their eyes each time I came in stating, "I don't know what's wrong with you, the test we perform all come back negative." They couldn't admit me because they didn't have a diagnoses and they were afraid to give me anything *else because nothing so far had worked, so they had no idea what else to try. By this time I was so weak, it took all I could do just to stand up (but still through it all... I knew there was a plan, God had not brought me through all these things just to let me die without me ever knowing the lesson. My mother had been staying with me but of course she too had things she needed to handle of her own, so I told her I would be alright. You know, when you're all alone and already weak that's when satan preys on you the hardest. There I was, sitting in the recliner and satan started to talk to me, "If you took all those sleeping pills, you would drift off to sleep and all this anguish would end." He reminded me how many long days and nights I had been grasping for air; how there was no cure for me; how even the many specialist I had seen couldn't help me; and finally he said, "You're going to die anyway!" I took the bottle of pills and dumped them all in my hand and as I picked up the glass of water I looked at all the pills in my hand and I began to crying out to the Master, "Why have you allowed this to happen to me, I have tried hard to serve you, even through all this I held on to you, because I knew you had a plan. You see I can't go on any longer and you said you would not put no more on us than we could bare. **I can not do it any more... HELP ME!**"*

*At that moment as I yielded my entire self over, not holding anything back, but giving it all up to be free, The Voice of Truth spoke, "**I AM GOING TO DO A <u>NEW</u> THING AND I NEED SOMEONE WHO'S WILLING AND STRONG ENOUGH TO ENDURE UNTIL THE END. I HAVE CHOSEN YOU. I NEED SOMEONE WHO IS WILLING TO LET ME LEAD.**" LATER, **THE VOICE SAID, "AS THE LINES IN YOUR HANDS ARE PLENTIFUL SO SHALL YOU PROSPER... AS YOU ALLOW YOURSELF TO BE USED BY GOD AND DO HIS WILL.**" At that moment I knew what the question (lesson) was and my answer was... Yes! Yes! Yes Lord. So from that day on, I have continued on my journey through life's mystical maze with a revelation in my heart and a new attitude in my spirit.*

Father God, first I reference you as the one and only true God. I thank you for everything that you've done, doing, and shall do for us, your people. Forgive us Oh God for we fall short of your glory and we thank you for your love that allows us to get back up and try again. Father God, do for others what you've done for me. I pray that they will allow you to help them to endure, so that they too can

Gloria Waters

receive the revelation that will help them to endure to the end.

May The Peace Of God Be With Us Always...
God Bless You.

PERSONAL LIFE-LESSON JOURNAL

FROM ME TO YOU

Gloria Waters

GOD BLESS YOU

DATE _____
ENTITLED_____
_____

Gloria Waters

DATE _____

ENTITLED_____

_____

DATE _____
ENTITLED_____

_____

DATE _____
_ENTITLED______
_____

DATE _____
ENTITLED_____

_____

Gloria Waters

DATE _____
ENTITLED_____

_____

DATE _____

ENTITLED_____

_____

Gloria Waters

DATE _____

*ENTITLED*_____

_____

The Love of My Life Swept Me Off My Feet THE GREAT I AM

DATE _____

ENTITLED_____

_____

Gloria Waters

DATE _____
ENTITLED_____
_____

DATE _____

ENTITLED_____

_____

Gloria Waters

DATE _____

_ENTITLED______

_____

DATE _____

ENTITLED_____

_____

Gloria Waters

DATE _____

ENTITLED_____

_____

The Love of My Life Swept Me Off My Feet THE GREAT I AM

DATE _____

_ENTITLED______

_____

Gloria Waters

DATE _____
*ENTITLED*_____

_____

DATE _____

ENTITLED_____

_____

Gloria Waters

DATE _____

ENTITLED_____

_____

DATE _____

*ENTITLED*_____

_____

Gloria Waters

DATE _____
ENTITLED_____
_____

DATE _____

***ENTITLED*_____**

_____

Gloria Waters

DATE _____
ENTITLED_____
_____

DATE _____

ENTITLED_____

_____

DATE _____
ENTITLED_____
_____

DATE _____

ENTITLED_____

_____